Back-to-School
IDEA BOOK

GRADES 2–3

MIND MOTION™

TREND enterprises, Inc.

Dear Teacher,

You are about to embark on an exciting experience that will inspire both you and the children in your group! Whether you are beginning another incredible year in teaching or meeting your own class for the first time, you will certainly have many exciting challenges.

One of the most important challenges is getting to know each child in the group. As you know, getting to know a new group of children or a child who joins your group during the year is more than just putting faces with names on a list. You'll want to know what makes each individual tick, what is special about each one, and what each will need from you to have a successful year. This *Back-to-School Idea Book* will help you get started. The activities will help you build a well-rounded curriculum to use during the first several weeks of school, at any time during the year when you add a new child to the group, or when you feel you want to build a sense of community in your group. You'll learn about each person's likes and dislikes, find out where individuals excel or have difficulty, discover how individuals relate to each other and to you, and much more.

Use the activities in this book to really get to know each child in your group. The activities relate to the subjects you deal with throughout a regular day or week. They are sure to add to your success as a teacher.

HAVE FUN!

2

Contents

How to use this book

To help you construct your lesson plans, this book includes several organizational strategies:

Preparation and materials needed are listed at the beginning of each activity.

The activities are organized by **length of time:** Short (5–15 minutes), Medium (16–45 minutes), and Long (46 minutes or more).

The top of each page shows **icons** that indicate the curricular areas to which the activity relates.

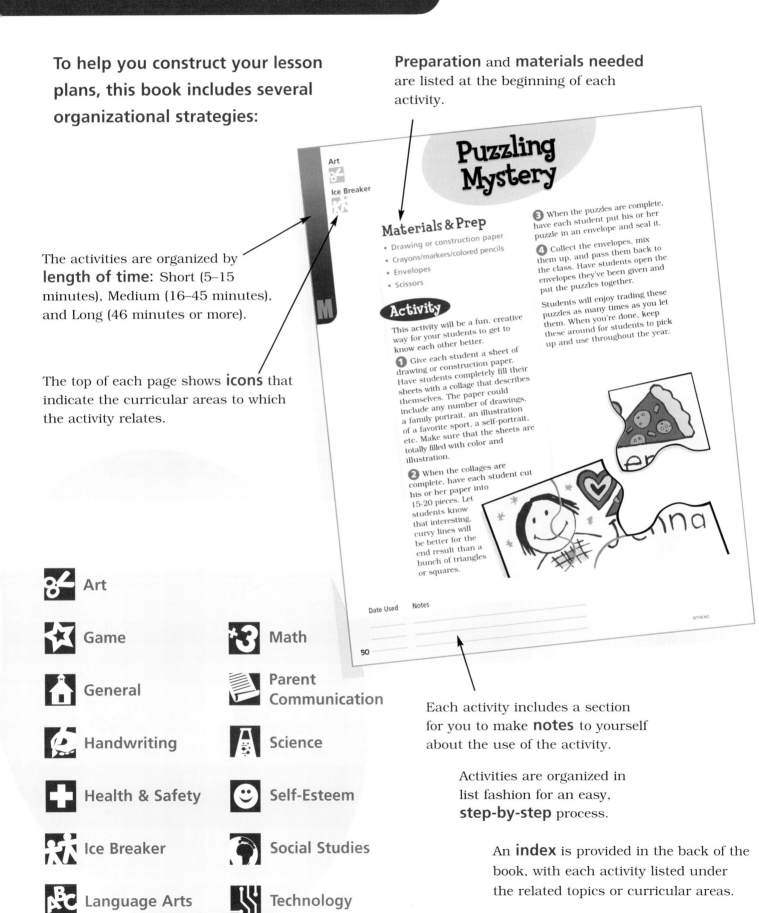

Each activity includes a section for you to make **notes** to yourself about the use of the activity.

Activities are organized in list fashion for an easy, **step-by-step** process.

An **index** is provided in the back of the book, with each activity listed under the related topics or curricular areas.

Art

Game

General

Handwriting

Health & Safety

Ice Breaker

Language Arts

Math

Parent Communication

Science

Self-Esteem

Social Studies

Technology

Making Pairs, Groups, and Teams

You are constantly trying to foster a sense of **community** and teach students the merits of **cooperation**. One way to do this is to have students work in pairs, groups, or teams. Organizing students into groups can be a very difficult and trying task. Gone are the days of "Captains" picking teams and numbering off "1, 2, 1, 2..." Today's children seem to be more sensitive, and certainly much too smart, for those old strategies. Listed below and on the following pages are some new ways to combine your students. Try the ideas to create random pairs, groups, or teams in fun ways that suit many of your classroom needs.

Playing Cards

Here are a few ways to use playing cards to create groups. You'll probably think of many other ways too. If you have more than 28 kids, adjust as needed.

- To get seven groups of four students each, mix and pass out all four eights, nines, tens, jacks, queens, kings, and aces. Have students find others with the same value cards.

- To get four groups, pass out equal numbers of each suit, such as seven diamonds, seven hearts, seven spades, and seven clubs. Have students find others with the same suit.

- To get pairs, pass out two of each card plus the jokers: two aces, two kings, two queens, two jacks, two jokers, etc. Have students find others with the same card.

Greeting Cards

Greeting cards are an excellent item to save and use in your classroom. To use them to create pairs or groups try these activities.

- Cut greeting cards in 2–,3–,4–, or 5–piece puzzles. Have students put puzzles together to find their groups.

- Get several greeting cards for different holidays, as many holidays as you want groups. Pass them out and have students form groups according to the holiday represented on their cards.

ABCs and 123s

Students' names and ages are very important to them. Try these five ideas for grouping.

- Group students by the first letter in their first or last names.

- Group students by having them find five other people who all have different first letters of their first or last names.

- Use third letters in names, last letters in names, or double letters in names.

- Use birthday dates or months to group students (January = 1, August = 8).

- Assemble all seven-year-olds in one place and all eight-year-olds in another. Then have them find someone in the other group for a partner.

Make Teams with Teams!

Gather several full team sets of baseball, football, basketball, or other team trading cards. When you have the card sets, try these ways to create groups.

1. All the Pitchers

Hand out the necessary number of cards in as many positions as you would like groups. For example, to make groups of five in a class of 30, pass out five each of six different positions: five pitchers, five catchers, five first basemen, five second basemen, five shortstops, and five third basemen. Then have the students find the people holding the cards with a player who plays the same position as the player on their cards.

2. Make a Team

Pass out the necessary cards for students to create teams of players. Students can match uniforms to find their other team members.

3. Cover Your Bases

Pass out cards from different teams for several positions, as many positions as you want students in a group. Have students find others with cards to complete a full team of players. For example, tell students they must find a pitcher; catcher; first, second, and third basemen; shortstop; and three outfielders. This creates equal groups of nine. If you would like smaller teams, try only using infield players. You could also use trading cards from another sport, such as basketball, which only has five team members on the court at a time.

Choose Your Favorite

Have students choose the things they like and form groups at the same time. This way they'll be in groups and already have something in common with everyone there! To get started, designate different parts of the room for the different options and have students go to the appropriate area. Or, you could graph the options and then have the class split up afterwards. Remember to provide as many options as you would like to have groups. Possible questions may include the following options:

- What is your favorite fast food restaurant?

- What type of pet do you have? (One option is none.)

- What is your favorite sport?

- Which cartoon character do you like the best?

- What is your favorite soft drink?

- Where would you like to vacation?

- Which television show do you like the best?

Families

Pair students by using their families as a vehicle. This important topic can be used as a fun pairing activity.

1. Siblings, Siblings

Have students move to one part of the room if they have a sister, another place if they have a brother, and another place if they don't have any siblings. If they have one of each, use those students to balance the groups, or make them a separate group.

2. Oldest, Middle, Youngest, Only

Separate students using relative position in the family as a grouping technique. Once they are in these groups you can keep them as is or pull one from each group to form the final groups. This can help to even out your groups with leaders, followers, etc.

My favorite fast food restaurant is...

Curriculum Connection

Use the curriculum as a vehicle to form pairs, groups, and teams. The following techniques will reinforce the curriculum and provide fun ways for students to find their place for the next exciting activity.

1. Math

Are you working on multiplication or division facts? These concepts are perfect ways to connect students. Write problems on one set of index cards and answers on another set. Pass the cards out and ask students to make correct problem-answer matches. If you want groups of five, write five different problems that all equal the same answer. Have students find others with identical answers.

2. Language Arts

Use language arts skills to find pairs and teams. Have students pair up by matching index cards—one set with book titles and another set with the authors or illustrators. Prepare synonym cards and make groups by having students find others who have synonyms of the word on their cards. You can gather groups by giving each child one letter on a card and have him or her find the other students with whom they can create a word.

3. Social Studies

The social studies curriculum provides endless possibilities for pairing and grouping. Give half of your students a state and the other half a capital and have them make matches. You can also match countries and capitals. You may also give students names of people in history and have them find other people who worked for the same cause, such as Martin Luther King, Jr., Rosa Parks, and Malcolm X.

Clothing

Are your students wearing buttons, zippers, snaps...? Use their clothing as a means for dividing them into groups.

1. Layers and Sleeves

Are half of your students wearing short sleeves and the other half wearing long? How about layers? Are some wearing only a T-shirt while others sport a T-shirt and a sweatshirt, or button-down shirt and a sweater? Layers and sleeves provide great possibilities for making groups.

2. Fasteners

What types of fasteners are on your students' shirts? How about students' shoes? It's easy to divide kids in many ways using this as a grouping technique. Have the kids with buttons go to one area, those with zippers to another, and students with no fasteners in another area. It's fun to have them compare and find their correct spots.

I have a backpack with a zipper!

Multiple Intelligence Learning Centers

Learning centers, based on Howard Gardner's theory of Multiple Intelligences, emphasize students' abilities, rather than inabilities. Children are challenged in areas where they are comfortable, and gently guided to work on intelligences they need to develop. Introduce one center a day and allow students to spend time exploring the activities and learning about the intelligence. Specific tasks geared to your curriculum can be added to the centers at any time. Each of the centers requires different materials. The materials you need will depend on the activities you choose to include.

Word Smart

The Verbal-Linguistic Intelligence Center

Children with strong word smarts love reading, writing, telling stories, and playing word games. When putting together your Word Smart Center, include activities that allow students to explore language, writing, and reading. Here are some ideas of what to include at the Word Smart Center:

- Writing materials, such as pencils; colored pencils; pens; markers; and many types of paper for creating books, including stationery, envelopes, notebook paper, and construction paper.
- A variety of reading materials: big books, library books, magazines, newspapers, crossword puzzles, dictionaries, books related to themes, poems, books with tapes, CD stories, and reference material on computer software. Encourage students to write books and have them "published" for the classroom collection.
- A computer with word processing, bookmarked Internet sites, and software programs that reinforce vocabulary with word games and word searches.
- Word charts and word webs used for building vocabulary and specific themes.
- Many kinds of pointers to make the study of words more fun, such as wands, flyswatters, frames, and flashlights.
- Feature an Author of the Month.
- Commercially made word games, such as Boggle, Chip-O!™, Prof. Wacky's Wahoo Word Lab™, or other popular games.

Body Smart

The Bodily-Kinesthetic Intelligence Center

Children strong in body smarts think and learn through physical movement and by touching and feeling. They are active and athletic, and may enjoy a variety of activities, including dancing, creative dramatics, running, jumping, building, sculpting, weaving, touching, and gesturing. Here are some ideas of what to include at the Body Smart Center:

- Opportunities for playing charades, story telling with puppets, and making props.
- Ideas on how to adapt books and stories into their own plays.
- Recipes and ingredients to make dough and putty. This provides practice in reading and following directions.
- Construction materials such as wooden blocks, and Legos.
- Discarded telephones, radios, and computer components that students can safely take apart and look at. The kids will enjoy using tools like screwdrivers to inspect the "guts" of some items they see every day.
- Space to display student collections, such as a shell collection, when studying about the ocean.
- Computer games that improve manual dexterity.
- Commercial games like Jenga, Twister, and Guesstures.
- Sign language books and posters. Have someone who signs be a guest speaker.

Picture Smart

The Visual and Spatial Intelligence Center

Children strong in picture smarts think in terms of images and pictures. They love designing, inventing, drawing, visualizing, and doodling. Here are some ideas of what to include at the Picture Smart Center:

- Materials such as paint, paint brushes of all sizes, markers, chalk, crayons, colored pencils, scissors, tape, glue, paper of many sizes and colors, stamps and stamp pads, wallpaper samples, yarn, string, and newspaper.
- An easel for painting or drawing large pictures.
- An artist's painting, to encourage students to copy a particular technique.
- Illustrated children's books to study the illustrations and try the different techniques used by the artists.
- A tubful of recycled materials for imaginative play.
- Clay for sculpting.
- A mapping activity, such as drawing a map of one's home, block, or school.
- Jigsaw puzzles, or directions for making one from scratch.
- "How to draw" books to help reinforce following directions.
- Games, including Connect Four, Tic–Tac–Toe, and memory. Pictionary, another commercial game, can easily be adapted to words that go along with themes or skills students are working on.
- Origami paper and instructions.
- Directions for students to illustrate books and covers for stories they have written.

Number Smart

The Logical-Mathematical Intelligence Center

Students with strong number smarts think by reasoning; and they love experimenting, questioning, figuring out logical puzzles, and calculating. Often they are strongest in science and math. Here are some ideas of what to include at the Number Smart Center:

- A microscope, thermometers, magnifying glasses, pattern blocks, calculators, a balance, dominoes, counters, junk boxes for sorting, base ten blocks, geoboards, graph paper, measuring instruments, tangrams, play money, a clock, timer, dice, and spinners.

- Science books that contain experiments, such as *Kid Kapers* by Judith Blumer, *Scienceworks* by Ontario Science Centre, *Thinking Games* by Valerie Anderson, and *Mudpies to Magnets* by Robert Williams.

- Space for children to work together picking out experiments that look interesting to them, collecting materials needed, preparing for a pre-experiment conference with the teacher or adult volunteer, and then doing the experiment.

- An estimation jar. Children take turns bringing in items to fill the jar and then having others estimate how many pieces are in the jar.

- Brain-teaser books.

- Commercial games like Prof. Wacky's Neon Number Flash™, Clue, Monopoly, Checkers, Chess, or card games.

- Computer programs that relate to the logical/mathematical intelligence.

Music Smart

The Musical Intelligence Center

Students strong in music smarts think via rhythm, tone, timbre, and melodies. They love singing, whistling, humming, listening to music, playing instruments, and tapping their hands and feet. Music is used to commit things to memory, and help learn and reinforce concepts. Here are some ideas of what to include at the Music Smart Center:

- Cassette tapes or CDs with a variety of music genres.

- Cassette tapes or CDs of nature sounds, the rain forest, and ocean.

- Opportunities to make up new words for familiar tunes.

- An area where children can record their voices.

- A collection of rhythm instruments.

- Sound identification activities, such as identifying the instruments in music selections.

- Materials to make instruments by following the directions in books. The instruments can later be used as background music for a student play.

- Opportunities for students to play instruments for the class.

- The commercial game Simon that plays a set of notes coded by color.

- Keyboards to practice reading music or composing music.

Nature Smart

The Naturalist Intelligence Center

Students strong in nature smarts are in tune with nature. They may be able to identify different species of plants and animals and may know a lot about our natural environment. Being outdoors, hiking, camping, going on walks or bike rides, are some of the ways nature smart people enjoy spending their time. Here are some ideas of what to include at the Nature Smart Center:

- A microscope and slides of different organisms or plant life.
- Space to display items that students find, or collections they have of rocks, shells, leaves, etc.
- Field guides and other nature books.
- Cassette tapes or CDs of nature sounds.
- Drawing paper, markers, crayons, or colored pencils for drawing landscapes and still-life nature scenes.
- Tempera paints for printing pictures with items collected outside.

Self Smart

Intrapersonal Intelligence

Students strong in intrapersonal intelligence know about themselves and are in tune with their minds and bodies. These self smart people enjoy spending time alone with their thoughts, keeping a journal, and other solitary activities. Besides the activities on the previous pages,

here are some other activities that may occupy these students:

- A computer for searching the World Wide Web looking for information and topics of interest.
- Paper, cardboard, fabric, and other scrap materials for creating a homemade journal.
- A tape recorder for making recordings of original stories.
- Games such as solitaire, working on puzzles, or other individual games.
- Time to daydream.

People Smart

Interpersonal Intelligence

Students strong in interpersonal intelligence are excellent in groups. These people love to be around other people and are the life of the party. People smart individuals enjoy partner and group assignments, being in clubs, and simply spending time with different people. Besides the activities on the previous pages, here are some other activities that may occupy these students:

- Plays to perform for others.
- Opportunities to volunteer with the elderly or help other children.
- Time to plan and attend events or parties.
- Time to share experiences in front of the group and engaging in other speaking opportunities.
- Group games and puzzles.

Buddy Bingo

Materials & Prep

- Customized Bingo grids
- Small photo of each student (often provided by the photographer that does the annual school pictures)
- Bingo markers, plastic chips, or other small markers
- Index cards
- Glue stick

Prior to playing the game, you will need to create a Bingo grid with enough spaces to affix one student's photo in each square. If you don't have enough students to complete a square grid, fill in extra spaces with pictures of adults around school, such as the principal. Make two or three photocopies of this card. Then, rearrange the photos and make two or three more copies. Continue in this manner until you have made enough copies for each student in your class to have a Bingo board. Also, write each student's name on an index card.

Activity

Students will learn their classmates' names by playing a popular game.

1 Distribute Bingo cards and markers.

2 Decide what kind of Bingo students will be playing: horizontal, vertical, diagonal, four corners, an H, or any other version you choose to play.

3 Shuffle the name cards and begin calling out names one at a time. When a name is called, students cover that person's photo with a marker.

4 The first student to get a Bingo shouts "Bingo!" and wins the round. The prize for winning can be thunderous applause, a sticker or stamp, or the opportunity to be the next Bingo caller.

Playing the game will motivate students to learn each other's names very quickly at the beginning of the year. In addition, they will enjoy playing when there is time to spare throughout the year.

Date Used   Notes

Beary Good Manners

Materials & Prep

- A stuffed toy bear
- Small suitcase
- Notebook
- Pencil
- Crayons/markers/colored pencils
- Note to parents explaining the activity

Activity

Young students will love teaching a stuffed bear good manners, and writing about it too!

1 Put the bear, notebook, pencil, and crayons in the suitcase and show it to your students. Explain that this bear does not always have good manners. Ask the class if they would like to help teach him to be more polite.

2 Talk about examples of good manners and what we do when being polite. Tell the class that each week the suitcase will go home with a different student. While the bear is in their home, the student should think of one good manner to teach the bear, such as sharing or covering your mouth when coughing.

3 The notebook is the bear's journal. During the bear's stay at the student's home, the student, with parents help, makes journal entries to describe what the bear was taught and how it was taught. The journal entry should include what was done to teach the good behavior, as well as how the bear spent the week. For example, students could write about how they played games with the bear, gave the bear a bath, and took it to Grandma's house. Students may also include pictures and photos depicting the bear's activities.

4 After explaining the process to your students, write a similar explanation for parents and include a copy of it in the suitcase.

Students will hardly be able to wait for a turn! Have them report on their experience with the bear when they return to school.

FACT: The door to the cave of a hibernating bear will always be on the North slope.

Date Used   Notes

Catch That Sum!

Materials & Prep

- Plastic cups
- Ping-pong balls
- Dry-erase markers

Activity

Students will love this active way of practicing math facts. This quick, fun game can be used to practice any mathematical operation you choose.

1 Divide the class into groups of four to six students.

2 Give each group three plastic cups. Have them use a dry-erase marker to write a different number on each cup. Choose numerals that will work for your students' level or the specific topic you are working on, such as double digits, large numbers, or even negative numbers.

3 Give each team two ping-pong balls. Have them set the numbered cups close together on a desk, table, or the floor five to ten feet away. Put a loop of masking tape on the bottom of the cups to keep them from tipping. Team members take turns throwing balls until they have managed to get a ball in two of the numbered cups.

4 Using the two cups with balls in them, students then perform the math operation (chosen before hand by the teacher) with the numbers written on the cups. For example, if you announce the operation to be subtraction, the children must subtract the two numbers to get the answer.

5 The team members should agree on the correct answer and check it with you. Then students erase the numbers and write different numbers on their cups. It's time for another round.

This is an especially good game to use on those indoor recess days or when you have some extra time to fit in a neat change of pace!

Date Used   Notes

Flash Card Friends

Materials & Prep

- TREND *Make-Your-Own Flash Cards*
- Marker

Activity

This activity provides an opportunity to review letter sounds, help children recognize each others' names, and learn little facts about each other.

1 Write each child's name on a flash card and then laminate the cards. *Make Your Own Flash Cards* from TREND work well.

Depending on the grade level, you may choose to write only each child's first name, first and last, or just the last name.

2 Start out by having each child stand up when you show his or her name card. The rest of the class responds by saying "Hi, _____."

3 Try covering up part of the name as you hold it up and see if children can still recognize the name.

4 Each day, ask a question that the kids must answer as they see their names.

- What is your favorite color?
- When is your birthday?
- What is your favorite food?
- Who is your newest friend?
- What is your favorite subject in school?
- Name one fun thing you did this summer?
- What is your phone number?

These cards will come in handy for a host of other activities throughout the year:

- Have each student place his or her card in the "attendance basket" each morning to have a quick check of who is present.
- Use the cards to choose helpers or pick partners.
- Because the children can read each others' names, they help with tasks like handing back papers or checking lunch counts.

Date Used   Notes

_____   _____

_____   _____

Welcome Puzzle

Materials & Prep

- Construction paper or 8½" x 11" tagboard pieces
- Scissors
- Markers
- Envelopes

Activity

This is a great way to greet children on the first day of school and get them busy with a fun activity.

1 Write a message to each student on a piece of colored construction paper or tagboard. Use statements such as: Welcome to our class; I'm glad you are here; We're going to have fun this year; etc.

2 Cut each note into as many puzzle pieces as your students can handle and put each puzzle in its own envelope.

3 Put one envelope on each desk for the students to discover when they come in the door on the first day. On each envelope, or on the board, write these instructions:

Open the envelope.
It's from your teacher you see.
Put the pieces together and you'll find a special message from me!

From,_____

4 As the children enter the room have them follow the instructions to complete their puzzles. They will have something to do that immediately gets them involved and conveys a warm greeting from you.

Consider offering a small prize, stickers or a pencil, to students as they complete the puzzle. They'll have fun and "fit right in."

Date Used   Notes

What If?

Materials & Prep

- None

Activity

Here is a short activity that will get your students' imaginations flowing. In the days ahead, when you have a minute to spare, ask students to respond out loud to these "What If" questions with a sentence or two.

- What if it rained orange juice instead of water?

- What if we used ice cubes for money instead of dollar bills?

- What if you were born old and grew younger?

- What if we floated around as if in outer space?

- What if you never had to go to school?

- What if your parent was the President of the United States?

- What if television had never been invented?

- What if all your hair fell out?

- What if candy was healthy and vegetables were junk food?

- What if you got to run your class and make all the rules?

Have your students submit more "What If" questions to a box in your room for use when you have time.

Extension: Have students illustrate the "What If" question. Then display their works of art for others to enjoy.

FACT: What if most of the animals on Earth had six legs? They do! There are more than 10 quintillion bugs on earth!

Date Used   Notes

Parent Survey

Materials & Prep

- One copy of the parent questionnaire for each student
- Envelopes

Activity

An excellent way to find out about your students is to ask the folks who know them the best, their parents. It is always best to have some sort of communication with parents and guardians before the first parent-teacher conferences.

Address envelopes to your students' parents and send a questionnaire home with your students for their parents to fill out and return to you. Use the questions in the next column as the basis for your questionnaire. Add specific questions that relate to your school or classroom. Parents are usually willing to tell you about their sons or daughters, and will appreciate the fact that you are interested enough to ask for the information.

Dear Parent,

In order to get to know your child, I would like to gather some information from you. Please take some time to fill out this survey and return it to me in a sealed envelope. Share any information that you believe will help your child and me get to know each other and have a great year!

1. What are your child's general feelings about school?

2. How often do you discuss with your child what he or she is learning in school?

3. What social skills would you like to see your child focus on this year?

4. What educational skills would you like to see your child focus on this year?

5. In what ways can I make this the best possible school year for your child?

6. Do you have any other questions, comments, or concerns?

Please feel free to contact me any time you have a concern or need. I will do my best to make sure that we have the very best school year.

Thank you,_____,

Your child's teacher

Date Used   Notes

_____   _____

_____   _____

_____   _____

Write On!

Materials & Prep

- Large coffee can with plastic lid
- Small strips of paper (8½" x 2")
- Pencils
- Chalkboard or white board

Cover the coffee can with colorful paper and label it "Write On!"

Activity

Every student should read, write, and be read to each day. Finding books for you and your students to enjoy is fairly simple, and usually enjoyable. Coming up with writing ideas isn't always so easy. Why not have your students be the ones to come up with those last minute writing ideas, story starters, or journal entries?

Introduce your students to the idea of a "suggestion box" of writing topics. Show them the coffee can you have decorated and labeled "Write On!" At any time they can write an idea on a slip of paper for a story or other writing assignment and drop it in the can. During the year, when individuals or the class need an idea for creative writing, they can pull an idea from the can and use it as the topic of a story.

Start your "idea can" with a bit of class brainstorming to get the creative juices flowing. Ask for writing topics from the kids and list them on the board. You will probably need to contribute some ideas such as these:

A day in the life of a potato.

When I learn to fly I will...

If I were the teacher, I'd...

Juan knew it was his lucky day the moment...

Billy Jo leaned over to pick the flower, but instead found a...

My best friend is great because...

Now ask the students to contribute their ideas to the coffee can by writing ideas on slips of paper. At least once a week, draw an idea from the can for a writing activity. You'll have plenty of ideas to choose from in your can. The next time you put journaling up on the schedule, students will be buzzing about which of their ideas will be selected.

Date Used   Notes

Guess the Classmate

Materials & Prep

- 3" x 5" index cards
- Pencils

Activity

Here is a way to help you get to know your students as they get to know each other.

Give each student three 3" x 5" index cards. Have each student write one interesting fact about himself or herself on each card. Encourage the students to write something that the other students wouldn't necessarily already know about them. Collect the cards and mix them up.

The game can be played a number of different ways.

> I'm an excellent tree climber.

1 When you need a five-minute activity before the buses come or music class begins, try this activity. Read off one of the cards from the pile and have the students guess to which classmate that fact belongs. The first one to raise his or her hand and give a correct response wins. (Wins what? That's up to you.)

2 Another way to use the cards later in the year is in a one-on-one game. Two students stand next to each other. You choose a card and read it. The first of the two students to correctly identify which student wrote that card advances by choosing another student for the next card. See if one student can make it all the way around the entire class.

3 One more way to play is to divide the class into two or more teams. Have one representative from each team go to the board. When a card is read, the first person to correctly write the student's name and put down the chalk wins a point for his or her team.

For added fun, put in some clues about yourself. The students will be thrilled to learn something new about their teacher.

Date Used   Notes

Simon Says Succeed!

Materials & Prep

- One beanbag per student
- Chalkboard or marker board
- Chalk or dry-erase markers

Activity

By playing variations of a popular game, students will improve test-taking skills.

Tests often incorporate directional words (i.e. on top of, beneath). If students are not familiar with these directions, tests can get quite difficult.

1 Give each child a beanbag and play Simon Says. Use lots of prepositions in your directions. Some examples follow:

- Simon says put the beanbag in your desk.
- Simon says put the beanbag on the back of your hand.
- Simon says place the beanbag on top of your head.
- Simon says put the beanbag between your hands.
- Simon says put the beanbag behind your left knee.

2 For a variation, choose students to go up to the board in groups of four. Give each group a writing implement and directions such as these:

- Simon says write your name.
- Simon says underline the first letter of your name.
- Simon says circle the last letter of your name.
- Simon says put a box around one of the middle letters of your name.

By using the board, rather than pencil and paper, you will be able to provide immediate feedback.

If you play these games regularly, you will help students feel more comfortable with test taking.

Date Used   Notes

Number Roll

Materials & Prep

- Two dice for each student
- Lined paper, individual chalkboards, or white boards
- Pencils, chalk, or dry-erase markers

Activity

This is an easy way to assess the students' number sense while they are having fun. It can be played as a whole class activity, by groups, or individuals at a center. Use this activity at the beginning of the year to assess each student's ability to organize information, number sense, recognition of number chunks, and how they form their numbers.

1 Give each student one die and the writing utensils you would like them to use.

2 To play, the student rolls the die and writes the corresponding number on a sheet of paper or an individual chalkboard.

3 Keep rolling the die until all the numbers from one to six have come up and have been written. Then use the two dice together and continue rolling until all the numbers to 12 have been written.

4 Have students estimate how many times they will need to roll one die to get each number, one to six.

5 Then have them keep rolling two dice and adding the numbers until they get to 100. How long did it take?

6 Have students think of other math problems they could do with the dice while they learn as they play.

Without even knowing it, students will show you how much they know by this simple activity, and they will certainly have a good time doing it.

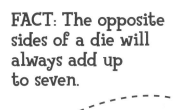

FACT: The opposite sides of a die will always add up to seven.

Date Used   Notes

Cube Graph

Materials & Prep

- One copy of the cube reproducible sheet for each student
- Markers/crayons/colored pencils
- Pencils
- Tape/glue/paste

Activity

This is a quick and different way to get to know each other and see at a glance how students in your classroom are alike and different.

1 Hand out one copy of the cube sheet to each student.

2 Direct the students to draw the information you request in the squares. Choose six items from the list below, or come up with some of your own, to direct the information that students will put on their cubes.

- Your first name written in bold letters
- Your favorite animal
- A picture of your favorite food
- A picture of a favorite book character
- Favorite subject in school
- The year you were born, written in large numerals
- Objects used in your favorite sport
- Favorite place to visit
- Proudest accomplishment

3 When students have finished filling in the cube, have them cut out the cube, fold it on the dashed lines, and glue the tabs to hold it together.

4 Now the fun begins. Students can share their cubes while you create giant graphs on the floor. The cubes will hold space for student selections. Graph student choices by stacking their cubes:
- What is your favorite pet?
- How many teeth have you lost?
- How many brothers and sisters do you have?

Throughout the year, you can use the cubes for picking partners and small groups, graphing opinions, voting on class and school-wide decisions, and in other inventive ways you and the students create.

Date Used   Notes

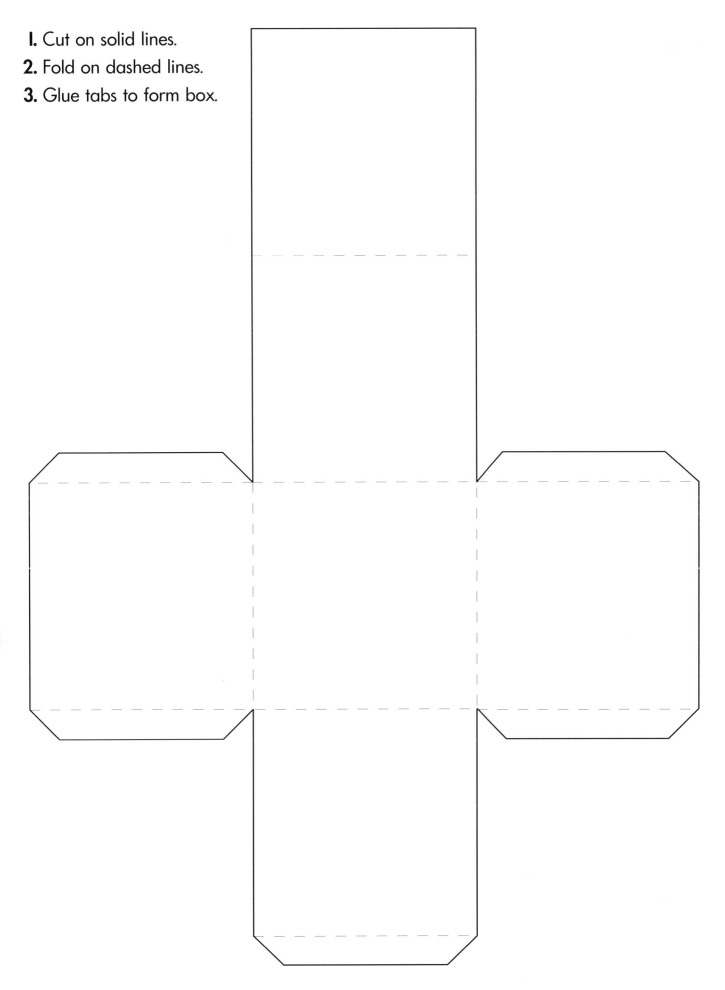

I. Cut on solid lines.
2. Fold on dashed lines.
3. Glue tabs to form box.

The Places You'll Go!

Materials & Prep

- Book, *Oh, the Places You'll Go*, by Dr. Suess

- "The Places You'll Go" reproducible

- Pencils

- Chart paper

Activity

Personal and group goal setting is a powerful tool to begin the school year. It will strengthen students' self-concepts and build classroom cohesion. It gives you a starting point and direction, as well as insight into each student.

1 Begin this activity by reading the popular book, *Oh, the Places You'll Go*, by Dr. Seuss. This book will surely delight and inspire your students.

2 Follow the story with a discussion about success. Use questions such as these: What is success? How does society define success? What would determine success for you personally? What would a successful school year be like?

3 Help the students realize that in order to achieve success they first have to define it for themselves.

It is only then that they can set goals toward that success. Continue with a discussion about goals. Have the students make the connection between setting goals and achieving success. How specific do you have to be when setting goals? How attainable should they be?

4 With your group, brainstorm whole-class goals. Write ideas on chart paper. Ask students: How can we be the best class this year? What will be our criteria for success? Settle on a few class goals, write them out, and refer to them throughout the year to check on progress.

5 Have students set their own personal goals for the school year. This could be done in journals the students keep or in letters kids write to themselves. The letters can be handed out at the end of the year or mailed to students' homes after the year ends. With students' permission, you may want to share the goals with parents at the first parent-teacher conference.

6 Have each student fill out a goal slip reproducible. Post these in the room for all to see. In this way, students can remember and share their special talents and goals.

Date Used   Notes

The Places You'll Go!

I, _____, bring special gifts and talents to my classroom, school, and community.

I know the goals for our class and have set my own personal goals.

X_____

I, _____, bring special gifts and talents to my classroom, school, and community.

I know the goals for our class and have set my own personal goals.

X_____

I, _____, bring special gifts and talents to my classroom, school, and community.

I know the goals for our class and have set my own personal goals.

X_____

I, _____, bring special gifts and talents to my classroom, school, and community.

I know the goals for our class and have set my own personal goals.

X_____

Planning Ahead

Materials & Prep

- Lined paper
- Pencils
- Markers/crayons
- Envelopes

Activity

"Welcome" is one thing every student likes and needs to hear when returning to school or entering a new classroom. Besides the usual ways to do this each year, try this idea at the end of the school year.

In the spring, have your class reflect on their year in your class. What did they like about it? What was their favorite memory? Who were their best friends? Once you have them in this reflective mode, have them write a letter to a new student entering that grade next year. This letter will be on the desks the following fall to welcome the new class to the room. Each letter will be individualized, created especially for the new occupant of that desk. The letter should include some of the following ideas and whatever else you choose to add:

- A big, friendly "Welcome!"

- An explanation of the class schedule.

- Information about their new teacher.

- Field trips and activities they can look forward to.

- A few thoughts about rules to follow.

- Information on class traditions.

- Anything else interesting or important.

You might want to ask a few students to write two letters just in case you have more students next year than this year. That way everyone can get a personal letter from a past student. If you have extras, use them for new students that enter your class throughout the year. Keep these tucked away until the first day of the new school year when you can then place one "Welcome" letter on the top of each desk in your room.

Welcome!

Date Used   Notes

Number Necklaces

Materials & Prep

- Large uncooked noodles (mostaccioli works well)
- String
- Scissors
- Fine-tipped, permanent markers
- Clear acrylic spray, available at craft and discount stores (optional)

Prior to this activity, write a variety of numbers and operational signs on noodles, one per noodle. Use fine-tipped, permanent markers and choose one color for numerals and another for operational signs. Choose the numerals and signs based upon your grade level. If you wish to preserve the noodles, you can spray them with a clear acrylic spray before students handle them.

Activity

Students will create wearable number necklaces that make number sense!

1 Distribute 18" lengths of string and have students create number necklaces by stringing the noodle numbers and signs in the correct order. (If students are having difficulty stringing the noodles, wrap a small piece of masking tape around the end of the string, or use shoelaces.)

2 Students put the noodles in numerical order, practice skip counting, or create equations. Challenge students to create equations whose answers correspond to a special number, such as their age.

After working so hard, students will be proud to show off their number necklaces!

Extension: Use the pasta and string to create number challenges. Students are to figure out the pattern or solve the equation. Let students create number challenges for other classmates to solve.

Date Used   Notes

Tic-Tac-Toe

Materials & Prep

- Physical education vests or papers with X's and O's on them for each class member

- Nine chairs

- Questions you have formulated on a topic you would like to review with your class

Activity

This familiar game can be used as a vehicle for reviewing and assessing many skills.

1 Decide what material you will review or use to challenge your students. It may be one of these topics:
- spelling words
- math facts
- mystery characters from a book
- review questions for a test
- trivia questions

2 Divide the class into two equal teams.

3 Teams should be easy to identify. Use team vests from the Physical Education Department or tape papers to each player's back marked with an X for one team and an O for the other team.

4 Arrange nine chairs in the traditional Tic-Tac-Toe pattern, and have each team sit or stand in a straight line near the chairs.

5 Decide which team will go first and then ask the first person in that line a question. If the student gives the correct answer, he or she may choose a chair. If the student answers incorrectly, he or she must go to the end of the line. Now it is the other team's turn.

6 The team that gets three people in a row horizontally, vertically, or diagonally wins the game.

The most exciting aspect of this game is the emphasis on the whole team, not each individual's answer. It is also an excellent way to review because all players will hear the questions and answers, helping them study one more time before the "big test."

Extension: To make the game last longer and add more strategy, add more chairs to create a larger "game board." Players would then have to get four or five in a row to win.

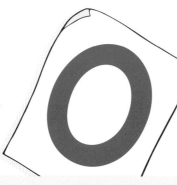

Date Used   Notes

Make Your Own Stationery

Materials & Prep

- One computer for each student
- Computer word processing or drawing program
- Computer clip art program (optional)

Activity

Personalized stationery is a wonderful thing for anyone to have for sending notes to a teacher, parents, or friends. This activity will allow the students to learn about the computer, while making their own page of stationery to be printed as needed throughout the year.

1 Have students open the word processing or drawing program you would like them to use. They may need to reduce the page to 50% size to see the whole page.

2 Encourage the students to create a border around the page being careful to allow for enough room to write when they use the stationery.

3 Have students type their names and whatever other information they want at the top of the page. Highlight, enlarge, bold, and center the type.

4 As an option, students can personalize the stationery with items from a clip art program or their own art.

Now each student has his or her own stationery to use throughout the year.

Date Used   Notes

Super Student Checklist

Materials & Prep

- One copy of the "Super Student Checklist" for each student

- Pencils

Activity

Beginning a school year is a big transition for students and teachers. There is a lot of new information to remember right off the bat: new schedules and rules, names of adults and new friends, as well as remembering to bring supplies to and from school.

This quick checklist for your students gives both student and teacher a look at what different skills need to be discussed and worked on. Remind students that items on the list that have not yet been accomplished become goals for the following week. Students can put a check mark by achieved items, draw happy or sad faces, or simply write yes or no to indicate a task has or has not been accomplished.

Try keeping the list for the next week and have the students see how they have improved. You and your students may want to use the extra lines at the end of the checklist to personalize it to fit your classroom needs.

If any of the checklist items become concerns throughout the year, pull out this sheet and have one or more students keep track for another week. It's a great way to see where the problems are and start to get kids back on track.

FACT: The average child spends twice as much time watching television than he or she does in school.

Date Used   **Notes**

Super Student Checklist

Name_____

**I came to school on time
every day this week.**

M T W T F

**I didn't give anyone a
"put-down" this week.**

M T W T F

**I remembered to bring
in all of my school supplies.**

M T W T F

I did all of my homework.

M T W T F

**I greeted my teacher and
classmates each morning.**

M T W T F

**I put my name on all
of my assignments.**

M T W T F

**I remembered to bring notes from home
and gave them to my teacher.**

M T W T F

**I remembered and followed the
rules of classroom behavior.**

M T W T F

**I was friendly to someone
I didn't know.**

M T W T F

_____

M T W T F

**I remembered my lunch
or lunch money every day.**

M T W T F

_____

M T W T F

Who's Who at Our School?

M

Materials & Prep

- Lined paper
- Pencils

Prior to doing this activity, you will need to prepare the staff in your building for a visit from your class.

Activity

It is important for each student to know that it takes more than a few people to run a school. This activity can easily help your students learn "who's who."

1 Take your students on a tour of the school. Introduce them to all of the adults in your building and have the adults tell the students what they do at school.

2 When you return to your room, or at a later date, make a list of all the staff members you visited and write their names in a column on the board. To the right of that, list all of the job titles in a mixed-up order to make a matching game. Have the students work in pairs or as a team to copy the list on paper and then match each person's name with his or her appropriate job title.

Example:

1. Mr. Gallivan	a.	Nurse
2. Ms. Naugle	b.	Counselor
3. Mr. Fellows	c.	Band Instructor
4. Mr. Latimer	d.	Assistant Principal
5. Mrs. Campbell	e.	Secretary
6. Mrs. Murray	f.	Custodian
7. Ms. Grant	g.	Computer Specialist

Knowing and recognizing the adults around will help to foster a sense of safety for your students.

Extension: Try having a "mystery person" show up at your classroom door to introduce himself or herself and tell about the job he or she does for the school.

FACT: Students in China go to school 251 days a year! Japanese students are in school 243 days per year.

Date Used   **Notes**

34

©TREND

Time Buddy Booklets

Materials & Prep

- Drawing paper
- Markers/crayons/colored pencils
- Pencils
- Construction paper in assorted colors
- Stapler

Activity

Students will create booklets about their buddies, showing what they do at different times during the day.

1 Start a class discussion by pointing out that while we are all different in many ways, we also do many of the same things every day. Brainstorm with your students to generate a list of daily routines, such as waking up, brushing teeth, eating breakfast, playing, doing chores, doing homework, watching television, and going to bed. Record this list on the board so students can refer to it while they work.

2 Next have each student create a book by folding four sheets of white drawing paper in half. Add a construction paper cover and staple the pages together.

3 Let students choose partners. The partners each create a book to illustrate and describe his or her buddy's day. Each page should say and illustrate one thing the buddy does. Include a clock drawing on each page to show what time of the day the activity occurs.

4 Students can also illustrate the covers with portraits of their partners.

With this fun activity, students get a chance to practice time skills and learn more about a friend! Display these booklets in the classroom for all to see.

FACT: Most Americans sleep 6-8 hours a day. This means the average person will sleep about 24 years of his or her life.

Date Used	Notes

Eat the Clock!

Materials & Prep

- White paper plates
- Pencils
- Two bags of chocolate chips or boxes of raisins

Activity

Students will love practicing telling time with edible clocks.

1 When showing students how to create a clock, you will want to demonstrate the process. Use a chalkboard or white board to show the students what a clock face looks like and to talk about the movement and purpose of the clock's hands.

2 Using paper plates as clock faces, have the children use pencils to write the numerals in the correct spaces. Show them that it usually works best to fill in the 12 and 6 first, then the 3 and 9 followed by the remaining numbers.

3 Next, pass out 24 raisins or chocolate chips to each student. Instruct them to put one or two by each number on the clock. Make sure students know to wait to eat the snack until you direct them to do so.

4 When you see that everyone is prepared, give the following directions:

- "Eat one treat where the hour hand is at 4:00."

- "Eat one treat on the number that is the hour you go to bed."

- "Eat one treat on the number that is two hours before 5:00."

- "Eat one treat on the hour that we get to school."

Continue in this manner until all of the treats are gone. You can "recycle" the clock faces by adding hands and using them for other activities.

Alien Science

Materials & Prep

- Stuffed animals (each child brings one from home)
- Paper clips
- Measuring tape for each student or pair of students
- Rulers/measuring tapes
- Lined paper
- Crayons/markers/colored pencils

Activity

Students will love using their science skills while they pretend to be aliens.

1 Ask each child to bring a stuffed animal from home. If you'd like to add some drama to this activity, you can ask them to bring either simple alien costumes from home or make alien masks at school.

2 Tell the students that they are to pretend to be alien scientists. Upon arriving from a distant planet, they find these odd stuffed creatures, which they think are the planet's only inhabitants. As scientists, they must gather information about the creatures.

3 Students first draw detailed pictures of their stuffed animals, labeling the alien's body parts.

4 Using either paper clip chains, measuring tapes, or rulers (depending upon skill level and availability), students measure the animals' body parts and record the measurements on their pictures.

5 Next, students choose three physical characteristics about their animals and make educated guesses about why the animals were designed in that way. For example, students may guess that an animal with a big snout can smell things far away, or that an animal with lots of thick fur came from a cold climate. Have them write these items on the bottom or back of their pictures.

6 Finally, display the stuffed animals and scientific papers about them.

Alien descriptions make a great Open House display!

FACT: The first animal to go into space was a dog named Laika.

Date Used	Notes

Class Calendar

Materials & Prep

- Copies of the reproducible calendar grid
- Pencils
- Overhead projector
- Calendar grid transparency
- Overhead markers
- Crayons/markers/colored pencils

Activity

This activity helps students learn more about the calendar and their classroom schedule.

1 Distribute the blank calendar grids and ask students to fill in the name of the month, the year, and the days of the week. Model the whole process on the overhead projector. This is a good opportunity to discuss the days of the week, the months of the year, and the seasons.

2 Have students fill in the dates on the calendar. Again, it is important to provide students with a model so that they begin the month on the correct day of the week. Add in any holidays. Have students lightly color the weekends and the holidays that are non-school days. Then at a glance, they can see which days are school days.

3 Next, have students record which days they go to art, music, physical education, and any other class they have outside of your classroom.

4 When the calendars are complete, students can tape them to the inside of their desks where they can easily refer to them. To keep your students on track, you may want to repeat this activity on the first school day of each month.

Extension: These calendars are ideal for quick math questions. When you have time at the beginning or end of classes ask students questions such as these:

- How many Tuesdays are in this month?

- What day of the week is September 23?

- What day comes before Sunday?

- What is the first day of the week?

- Is the third Thursday of the month on an odd or even numbered date?

- How many days until our next art class?

Date Used   Notes

Month _____

Year _____

Caught in a Brainstorm

Materials & Prep

- Paper strips
- Writing paper (optional)
- Pencils (optional)
- A hat

Before using this activity, prepare the paper strips by writing a category on each (see #1 below).

Activity

Get your students thinking with this fun brainstorming activity. This lesson will engage all students and get them to stretch their thinking and classification skills in a fun and imaginative way.

Things found in the jungle

Types of transportation

Musical instruments

1 Place the paper strips with different categories written on them into a hat.

Categories may include the following:

Things found in the jungle
Things found in the forest
Things found in the desert
Things found in the tundra
Foods that begin with A
Animals that live in the rain forest
Games people play
Types of careers
Things that float
Cities or towns in your state
Animals that live in the ocean
Types of transportation
Musical instruments
Things found on a playground
Things made of wood
Things that roll

Have a student draw a category from the hat. Then students take turns listing different items that apply to the category. Have a volunteer tally answers on the board.

2 As common answers dwindle, encourage students to dig deep to come up with more unusual items to add to the list. Remind students to try not to duplicate answers.

3 As an option, have students write their brainstorm ideas on paper, either working with a partner or on their own. Then compare lists and see how many answers they came up with that others did not.

This activity is an excellent time filler and can be used in any number of ways throughout the school year. Brainstorming is a valuable research tool, and each opportunity to practice will help students as they search for information throughout the year and beyond.

Date Used   Notes

School Mates

Materials & Prep

- Photos of each student and school staff member
- Index cards
- Rubber cement

Activity

Students will learn to recognize their classmates and school staff members while honing their concentration skills in this matching game.

1 Prepare this game by taking individual photos of each student in your class and school staff members. Take the film to a photo lab where they offer double prints for free. Mount each photo on a separate index card.

2 This game works best if students play it in groups of two, three, or four. Choose the groupings that work best with your class.

3 There are two ways students can play with these cards.

- The first way to play is for one player to shuffle all of the cards and spread them out face down on a table or floor. Each player in the group then takes a turn choosing cards to turn over in an effort to make a match. In addition to finding two identical photos, the student must name the pictured person in order to claim the match. Students who make matches get to continue taking turns until they turn cards over that don't make a match or can't name the person in matching photos. The student with the most matches at the end wins the game.

- A little later in the year play the game in a similar manner, with a twist. Now they must take one of each picture out of the deck and replace it with a card with the student's name written on it. To make a match, students must match a photo with the written name of the person depicted.

Students will enjoy playing this matching game all year long!

Date Used   Notes

Sock Spelling

Materials & Prep

- Large socks
- Plastic or foam letters of the alphabet

Activity

Students will love this tactile letter game.

1 Place three to eight letters in a clean sock without revealing the letters to the class.

2 Have students take turns reaching into the sock, feeling the letters, and guessing what letters are in there. You may also tell the students what letters are in the sock and have a student pull out the letter you designate.

3 Then remove all the letters and have groups of kids make as many words as possible with the letters. You might want to use letters from words on the class spelling list as a way to get in some extra review.

4 To make the activity a game, divide students into two teams. Using two socks with letters, let one member from each team simultaneously work on words. See which team can make the most words with the letters in the sock.

Your students will have fun with these word-building activities and will hardly realize that they are learning more and more.

FACT: Knitted socks were discovered in Egyptian tombs dating as far back as the third century A.D.

Date Used   **Notes**

Friendship Books

Materials & Prep

- *Frog and Toad are Friends* by Arnold Lobel
- *Who Will Be My Friend?* by Syd Hoff
- *Do You Want To Be My Friend?* by Eric Carle
- Chart paper
- Markers

Activity

In this activity, students will learn about friendship through literature. Over the course of a few days, read the books listed above to the class. If you have a favorite book that highlights friendship, read that book as well. After reading each book, have a class discussion about friendship.

1 Have the students name the main characters of the book and list them on chart paper.

2 Underneath each character's name, list the traits that suggest he or she is a good friend. For example, under Frog's name from *Frog and Toad are Friends*, students could list that he is helpful, hardworking, and wise.

3 If any characters have negative characteristics, you can record those, too, using a different colored marker. For instance, students might note that Toad is lazy.

4 After discussing each book, have students read the positive traits with you. Then have them think of a classmate who possesses one or more of those traits.

5 Give students an opportunity to compliment the person they named by saying something like this, "Julia is a good friend because she is helpful like Frog."

This activity is a great way to bring meaning to books, as well as promote friendship among students.

Date Used   Notes

Hoop It Up!

Materials & Prep

- Two 12' lengths of rope
- Venn Diagram reproducibles (copy double sided)
- Markers/crayons/colored pencils
- Magazines (optional)
- Glue/paste (optional)

Students will learn more about Venn Diagrams and about each other in this dynamic activity.

1 Start by laying two rope circles side by side with a few inches of space between them.

2 Choose eight students to stand near the circles. Ask those with brothers to stand in the left circle. Then ask those with sisters to stand in the right circle. It may help to label the circles with index cards.

3 At this point, a student may point out that she or he has brothers and sisters (especially if you purposely choose a participant who has siblings of both genders). Ask your students how to deal with this problem. Can anyone figure out how to include this person in the activity? Of course, to "fix" the problem all you need to do is overlap the circles so the person with both a brother and a sister can stand in the area that overlaps.

4 Now you can make several more life-sized Venn Diagrams by asking different questions that will help you and your students learn more about each other. Try these questions:

- Whose family has a car? Whose family has a truck or van?
- Who likes pizza? Who likes spaghetti?
- Who has a cat? Who has a dog?

5 Students can use the reproducible sheet to create their own Venn Diagrams. You can give them topics, such as things that are red and things that are blue, or things that are plastic and things that are metal. Have students draw pictures, use words, or use magazine pictures to fill in their diagrams. After completing some diagrams where you have chosen the category, they will probably be eager to choose and illustrate some of their own categories.

Date Used   Notes

Venn Diagrams

Name _____

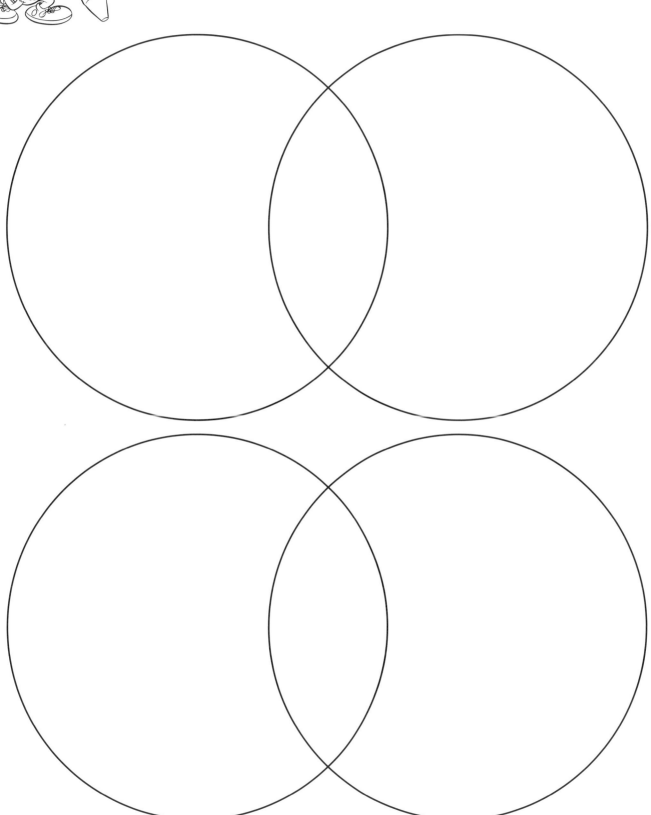

Cartoon Hunt

Materials & Prep

- Computers equipped with Internet access and printers
- Computer disks
- Writing paper
- Pencils

Activity

Students will love hunting for their favorite cartoon characters on the Internet!

1 Before doing this activity you will need to show your students how to connect to the Internet and use search engines to locate information on the World Wide Web.

2 Have your students, either individually or in pairs, connect to the Internet.

3 Ask each one to use a search engine (i.e. Lycos, Yahoo, Excite) to find a picture of a favorite cartoon character. Do any necessary screening of Web sites before you do this activity.

4 Next have students save the image to a disk and print it. Then have them create comic strips or write stories using the character.

5 Finally, be sure to teach your class how to exit the Internet and correctly shut down the computers, if necessary.

It is usually easy for students to learn computer skills. These Internet searching skills will come in handy throughout the year.

FACT: Mark Hamill, Luke Skywalker in the movie Star Wars, has provided the voices for over 400 cartoons since he made the movie.

Date Used   Notes

Round Robin Math

Materials & Prep

- Lined paper
- Pencils

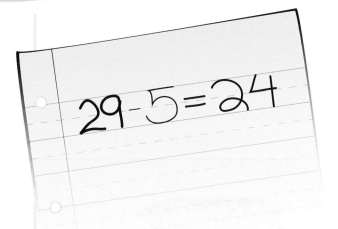

$$29 - 5 = 24$$

Activity

This is a great way to briefly assess your students' math skills at the beginning of the school year, as well as a fun, quick time filler at any time during the year.

1. Arrange students in groups of five. Tell them that each person will contribute one part of an equation.

2. The first student writes a number, such as 29, and passes the paper to the next child.

3. The second child writes an operational sign, such as –, and passes the paper.

4. The third student writes another number, such as 5; that when applied in the equation, will not result in a negative number, and passes the paper.

5. The fourth student writes an equals sign and passes the paper.

6. The fifth student writes the answer (24).

7. To build cooperation skills with your students, require teams to all agree that the equation is correct before moving on to create another equation. Make sure that every student has a chance to write each part of the equation.

As you circulate around the room, it will become apparent to you which students need to work on their computational skills. To turn this into a competitive game, see which team can create the most correct equations in a set period of time. Students will have so much fun, they won't realize this is a learning drill!

Date Used   Notes

Don't Break My Heart

Materials & Prep

- One large piece of red construction paper
- Scissors
- Markers

Before the class arrives, cut a large heart out of construction paper.

Activity

This activity reinforces respect for other's feelings. With very little teacher input the finished product dramatically illustrates how important it is to respect the feelings of others.

1 Take out the heart that you cut from the construction paper and ask each student to sign it.

2 Ask each student to make a statement that might hurt a person's feelings. With each response, crumple a little more of the heart you are holding. When all of the children have responded, the heart should be in a small ball.

3 Next, have each child say something that would make a classmate feel good. With each positive comment, open a little more of the heart.

4 When the students are finished, the heart is back to normal—almost.

5 Discuss the heart with your students. Why are there still wrinkles in it? Do they ever go away?

Display the heart in a prominent place in your room for the year. Throughout the year, refer back to the heart when there are playground conflicts or conflicts over sharing.

Julia
Emma
Mathew
Ian
Kristen

Date Used   **Notes**

©TREND

I Will Follow You...

Materials & Prep

- Jar of peanut butter
- Jar of jelly
- Loaf of bread
- Six butter knives
- Napkins or paper towels

Activity

This is an uproarious way to demonstrate the importance of following directions.

1 Use your best acting skills to pretend that you forgot how to make a peanut butter and jelly sandwich. Ask the students to give you step-by-step instructions, promising to follow them faithfully.

2 As you are working, have a volunteer copy the directions given onto the chalk/white board. Interpret the directions very literally, as the example illustrates. If students discover errors in their directions, allow them to revise. Continue until you have successfully completed the task.

Here is an example of how some of the discussion might go:

- Student: "Spread peanut butter on the bread."

- Teacher spreads peanut butter all over the bread bag.

- Student: "No! Take two slices of bread out of the bread bag and spread peanut butter on them."

- Teacher removes two slices of bread and spreads peanut butter all over the crust edge.

- Student: "Oops, spread the peanut butter on the white, flat part of the bread."

3 Once everyone agrees that the directions are accurate, ask for volunteers to help you make more sandwiches so that everyone can have a half of a sandwich if they would like.

4 While you and your helpers are busy, have the rest of the students work on giving directions to their friends for some everyday tasks, such as brushing teeth, tying shoes, or washing hands. The listener can pantomime the directions as they are given. Ask them to evaluate each other's directions to tell if they would be able to accomplish the task or not.

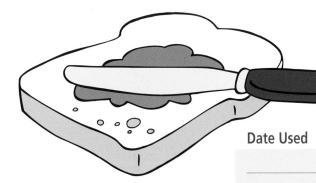

Date Used	Notes

Puzzling Mystery

Materials & Prep

- Drawing or construction paper
- Crayons/markers/colored pencils
- Envelopes
- Scissors

Activity

This activity will be a fun, creative way for your students to get to know each other better.

1 Give each student a sheet of drawing or construction paper. Have students completely fill their sheets with a collage that describes themselves. The paper could include any number of drawings, a family portrait, an illustration of a favorite sport, a self-portrait, etc. Make sure that the sheets are totally filled with color and illustration.

2 When the collages are complete, have each student cut his or her paper into 15-20 pieces. Let students know that interesting, curvy lines will be better for the end result than a bunch of triangles or squares.

3 When the puzzles are complete, have each student put his or her puzzle in an envelope and seal it.

4 Collect the envelopes, mix them up, and pass them back to the class. Have students open the envelopes they've been given and put the puzzles together.

Students will enjoy trading these puzzles as many times as you let them. When you're done, keep these around for students to pick up and use throughout the year.

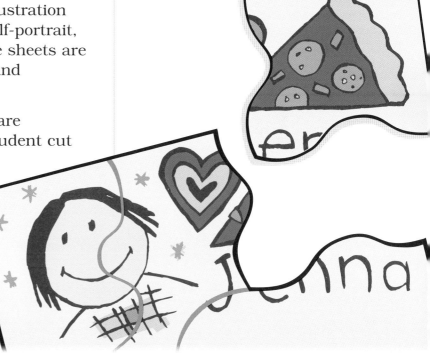

Date Used   Notes

©TREND

Place Mat Shuffle

Materials & Prep

- Solid color fabric place mats (purchase these or call upon parent volunteers to make them)
- Art smocks
- Fabric paint and/or fabric markers
- Newspaper
- Paint brushes and water containers
- Paper towels or paint rags

Or

- Poster board cut into the place mat size of your choice
- Markers
- A laminating machine or clear contact paper

Gather enough fabric place mats, or cut enough poster board pieces, so that each student can make his or her own place mat.

Activity

Students will enjoy creating their own place mats, which can then be used to help make new friends.

1 Protect work surfaces with newspaper, and clothing with art smocks. Talk about how place mats are used. Then give students the materials to decorate a place mat for themselves. If you have fabric place mats, discuss how to use the paint to avoid getting it on clothes.

2 Allow students to express their individuality on their place mats, requiring only that their names be clearly visible. If using poster board, laminate the finished products or cover them with clear contact paper before use.

3 Next, add "Place Mats" to your list of student helpers. The place mat person's job will be to go to the lunch area a few minutes early and set up the mats. Now everyday when your students go to lunch, everyone will have a place to sit that is just for them.

As the students rotate through this job, you can be assured that your students' seats will be continuously rearranged at lunch, insuring that they will get a chance to know all of their classmates.

Date Used   Notes

My Time Capsule

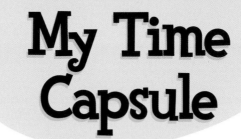

Materials & Prep

- Two copies of the "Time Capsule" reproducible for each student

- Pencils

- Something to hold students' "Time Capsule" sheets: tubes from wrapping paper or paper towels, etc.

- Tape

- Construction paper (optional)

- Markers/crayons (optional)

Activity

This activity provides a fun way for the students to get to know each other. It also gives you a quick reference to students' skill levels as they start the year.

1 Have the children fill in the "Time Capsule" sheet with information about themselves. Use the information to get to know one another in class.

2 Then, seal the sheets inside a container to be opened the last week of school. Potato chip cans, gift wrap tubes, or paper towel tubes taped on the ends make great containers. Students may enjoy decorating the containers by wrapping them and adding fun pictures or art.

3 Before opening the time capsules during the last week of school, have students fill in a second "Time Capsule" sheet to see how much they have changed over the year. At the end of the activity talk to your students about how much things change over a year. Discuss other changes that have gone on in the community or world over the past several months.

Date Used   Notes

My Time Capsule

This is a record of my life on ___/___/___

Name _____ Age ____

My address _____

_____

* My best friend _____

* My favorite food _____

* My favorite song _____

* My favorite color _____

* My favorite book _____

* My favorite game _____

* My favorite place to visit _____

* My favorite sport _____

* My best subject _____

* I would like to improve _____

* I would like to learn about _____

_____

_____

Bus Rules

Materials & Prep

- 12" x 18" orange or yellow construction paper
- Red and black construction paper
- Metal brads
- Scissors
- Glue/paste
- Crayons/markers

Activity

Bus safety is a big topic. It is important to discuss bus rules with your students at the beginning of the year so they will be prepared to ride safely on their way to and from school or on fieldtrips. By putting students in charge, this activity will help you put a little twist on the regular rule announcements. When students make the rules, often they are tougher than those you would make.

1 Hand one orange or yellow sheet of paper to each student. Ask them to fold it in half by making a "hamburger fold" in the paper.

2 Holding the paper fold side up, cut a square out of the upper right hand corner.

3 Round the top three corners to form the bus.

4 Cut the corners off a 3" x 3" red square to make a stop sign. Glue it to the bus.

5 Round the corners of two 4" x 4" black squares to make wheels. Attach them to the bus with the brads.

6 Allow students to draw the windows, door, and passengers.

7 After the children have completed the buses, have them gather around you to come up with the 10 most important things to remember when riding a bus. Type up their responses, make copies for everyone, and have them paste or glue the rules inside the buses.

An activity like this will make reading and remembering the rules seem much easier for your students, and will help to keep them safe.

Date Used   Notes

I'm Different!

Materials & Prep

- *The Sneeches* by Dr. Suess (video or book)

You will need to dress up for this activity so that your students can see you in some silly clothes. Wear mismatched clothing, a silly hat, different glasses, and any other items that will make you look different than normal.

Activity

Everyone thinks there's something they do that makes them stand out. The problem is that kids just want to fit in. This activity will give you a chance to act silly in front of your students and in the process, teach them a very valuable lesson.

1 Ask another teacher or assistant at school to greet your students in the morning and help them settle in. Have them begin the normal routine before you arrive.

2 Wait until class has started, and then enter the room acting goofy and apologizing for being so late.

3 Tell the students that you would like them to watch a video, or listen to *The Sneeches*.

4 When the story is over, ask students for feedback using the following questions: Name all of the things that were different about the two different groups of Sneeches. How did the two groups treat each other? Why do you think the Star Bellied Sneeches treated the Sneeches without stars the way they did? Do you think it was fair the way the Sneeches without stars were treated? How did the Star Bellied Sneeches feel when the Sneeches without stars could have stars put on their bellies? What did they do? What happened in the end when they couldn't tell one group from the other? Do you think people ever act like the Sneeches?

5 Next, pair up your students. Have each pair come up with at least five things about themselves that are different from each other.

6 Talk about how even though students are different—some wear glasses, some are of a different race, and some have curly hair— every one is just as important as everyone else and, everyone in the class is a potential friend.

Throughout the year let the Sneeches be an example of working to get along.

Date Used   Notes

Back to the Basics

Materials & Prep

- One copy of the "Food Guide Pyramid" sheet for each student

- Food Guide Pyramid reference material

- Crayons, markers, or colored pencils

- Lined paper

- Snack (optional)

Gather food samples to represent each of the food groups. Prepare small pieces for everyone to taste.

Activity

Introduce this activity by having samples of food from each of the areas of the Food Guide Pyramid (fruits; vegetables; meats and other protiens; dairy products; breads and grains; fats, oils, and sweets) for all students to taste. After sufficient tasting, follow these steps for a tasty activity that will help students understand how to eat well, while eating foods that they like.

1 Review or introduce the Food Guide Pyramid with your students. Brainstorm a list of all their favorite foods they enjoy at home, school, Grandma's, or at a restaurant.

2 Figure out where these foods fit into the pyramid categories.

3 Now have the students create their own Food Guide Pyramids on the reproducible sheet provided. Students can fill in each section of the pyramid with all of the foods they like to eat. Give students the option to draw pictures of the foods in each group.

4 On the back of the sheet, have students create a days worth of meals they would like to prepare or eat, including the necessary amounts of food from each group.

5 Read some of the meals to the rest of the class and have them raise their hands if they would like that meal too.

6 At the end of the activity, share a fun, easy, and healthy snack you like to eat with the students. This will give them a good idea of a snack they might be able to make for themselves after school.

FACT: The average child will eat 15 lbs. of cereal in one year.

Date Used   Notes

Food Guide Pyramid

Name _____

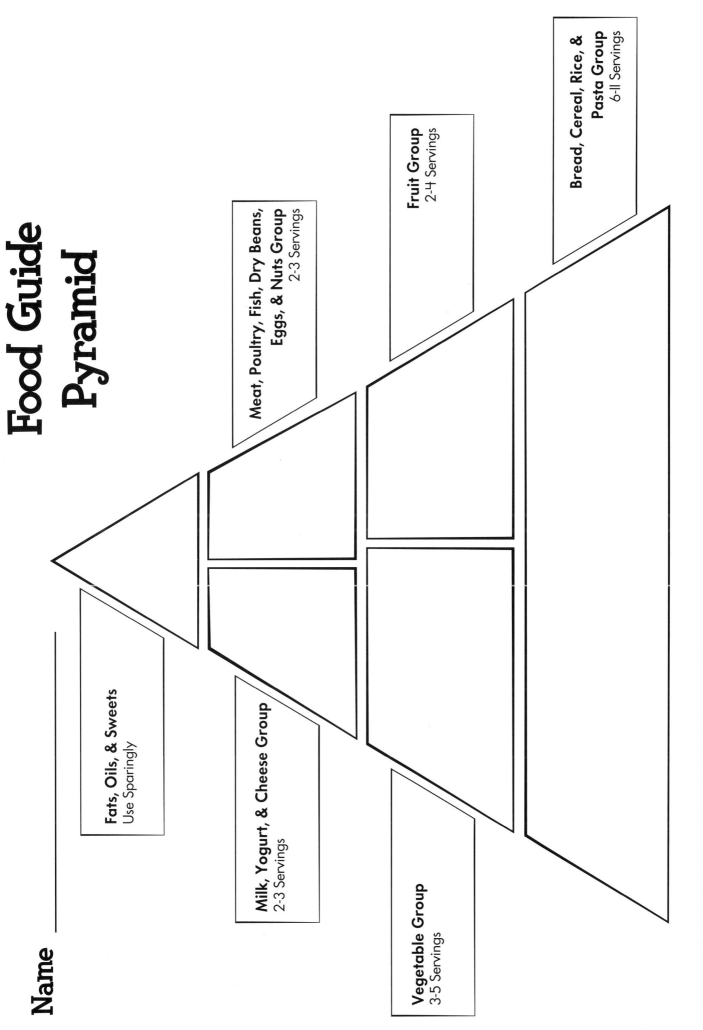

Fats, Oils, & Sweets
Use Sparingly

Milk, Yogurt, & Cheese Group
2-3 Servings

Meat, Poultry, Fish, Dry Beans, Eggs, & Nuts Group
2-3 Servings

Vegetable Group
3-5 Servings

Fruit Group
2-4 Servings

Bread, Cereal, Rice, & Pasta Group
6-11 Servings

Eat Your Words!

Materials & Prep

- Vegetable oil
- Creamy peanut butter
- Honey
- Nonfat dry milk
- Wax paper
- Large mixing bowl
- Measuring cups
- Plastic or metal spoons
- Wooden spoon

Activity

In this activity students will form letters out of dough. After the letters are made, the fun continues as the kids can eat the letters and words.

1 As a class, make at least two batches of edible dough, using the following recipe:

- 1 teaspoon vegetable oil
- 2 cups creamy peanut butter
- 1 cup honey
- 3 cups nonfat dry milk

Combine the ingredients and mix them thoroughly in a large bowl. The children can measure and add the ingredients. You can double or triple the recipe to suit your needs. Refrigerate the dough for one hour or until it is firm enough to handle. (Dough works best if used the same day.) While waiting for the dough, involve the class in other volume measurement activities.

2 Have students wash their hands. Then give each student a 12" x 12" square of wax paper and a small mound of dough. Let them use the dough to form letters. Each child can make one letter of the alphabet, or several letters and use them to spell his or her name or other words. Challenge a group to make a sentence with each person adding a word.

3 Of course, at the end of this activity, students get to actually eat their words!

Throughout the activity, be concerned about proper handling of the dough. Be sure hands and work surfaces are clean. Make it a point to talk about this with the students, making sure they understand that they are to eat only the dough they handle.

Date Used   Notes

Silhouette Collage

Materials & Prep

- 12" x 18" black construction paper
- Overhead projector
- Pencils
- Old magazines (at least one for every two students)
- Scissors
- Glue/paste

Activity

This art activity will boost self-esteem and creativity, and make a lovely display in your room.

1 Begin with pairs of students making silhouettes of each other. The best way to do this is to tape a sheet of construction paper vertically on the wall, at the height of the student. The student whose silhouette is being created stands with one shoulder to the paper. That student's partner turns on an overhead projector facing the student, creating a shadow on the black paper. The partner traces the shadow line with a pencil while the other student stands

still. Repeat these steps to create the other partner's silhouette on another piece of paper.

2 Have the students find and carefully cut out pictures or words from the magazines that describe themselves: favorite foods, places, activities, symbols, or words describing what they are like.

3 Cut out the silhouette and paste the magazine cutouts all over it. The pictures should overlap slightly, and cover much of the silhouette, except for a space at the bottom where kids should add their names.

Display these amazing works of art in your classroom or in a commons area in the school.

FACT: The silhouette on the Major League Baseball logo is Harmon Killebrew. The silhouette on the NBA logo is Jerry West.

Date Used	Notes

Spell-Binding Fun

Materials & Prep

- Pencils
- Notebook paper or computer
- Graph paper
- Copy of the class roster for each student

Activity

Kids love to see their names in print and everyone wants to have his or her name spelled correctly. To help everyone, use names for the first spelling list of the year. Throughout the week, use the following activities to help students learn the names and spellings. For an extra challenge, use last names as well.

1 Have your students try this jumble activity. On the board, sheet of paper, or on a computer screen, mix up the letters of a name to form a jumbled word. Leave a space under the jumbled word for the students to write the correct spelling.
(Example:
1. tujnis
[Justin],
2. zabetileh
[Elizabeth].)

2 Another fun activity is a crossword puzzle. On a sheet of graph paper, connect the names of the students across and going down the paper. Using another sheet of graph paper, draw boxes around the spaces with letters to make your crossword puzzle. Then, number the squares as you would a regular crossword puzzle, starting at the top left and numbering across and down the page. Now comes the fun part. Make up a clue for each student to correspond with the name in the puzzle.

3 One more spelling activity is Speed Word. This not-usually-quiet game involves two teams. Each team has one member go to the board. You say the name of a student on your spelling list. The first one at the board to correctly spell the name and put down the chalk or marker gets a point for his or her team.

Having students learn how to spell each others' names is an excellent ice breaker and will help everyone learn names. Students will also enjoy sharing information about themselves during the week to help others remember them!

Date Used   Notes

Kite Poems

Materials & Prep

- Pencils
- Lined paper
- Crayons/markers
- Drawing or construction paper
- Fabric, ribbon and/or crepe paper

Activity

This art project is also a lesson in poetry and the parts of speech. In addition, it is a good way to get to know your students and for them to get to know each other.

Before students begin writing, review adjectives, action verbs, and nouns. When students have a grasp of these concepts, have them create their own poem that fits this structure:

Line 1: your name

Line 2: two adjectives that describe you

Line 3: three action verbs having to do with you

Line 4: create two adjective/noun combinations

Line 5: three more action verbs

Line 6: two new adjectives

Line 7: your last name

Students should write their rough draft on scratch paper, edit and revise as needed, and then transfer it to construction paper for their final draft. The poem is in the shape of a kite. Write the example shown on the board to help kids visualize how their kite poems might look. Students use their creativity to make their kites unique, just like themselves, using markers, crayons, and other media. Ribbon, fabric, or crepe paper will make wonderful kite tails. Display the kites in your classroom by hanging them from the ceiling or creating a display on the walls.

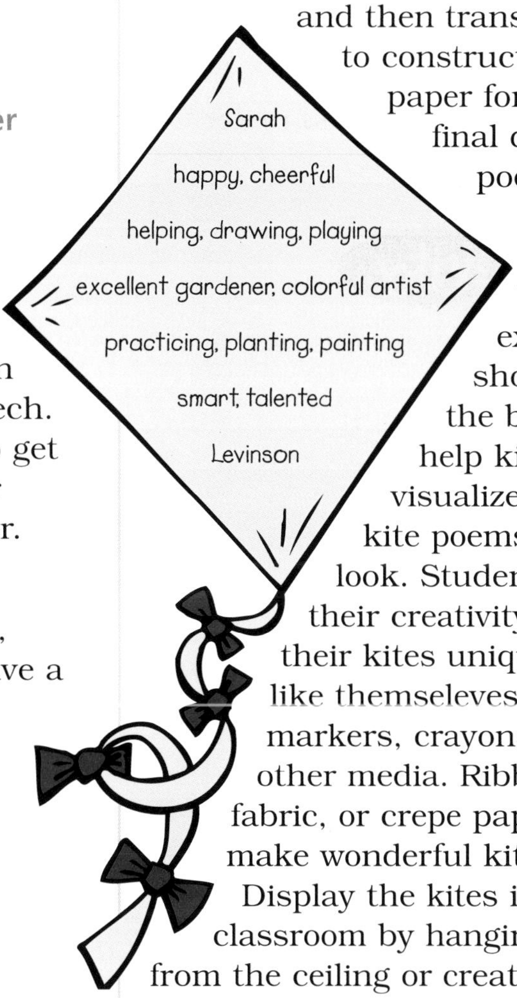

These works of art will be an excellent reminder of how every student can soar in your classroom!

(Kite illustration text:)
Sarah
happy, cheerful
helping, drawing, playing
excellent gardener, colorful artist
practicing, planting, painting
smart, talented
Levinson

Date Used   Notes

Shirt Tales

Materials & Prep

- Crayons/markers
- Cord or rope
- Clothespins
- One copy of the reproducible sheet for each student

Activity

Here is a fun and easy activity that will allow your students to really express themselves.

1 On the day you plan to begin this activity, have students wear their favorite T-shirts to school. Give each student an opportunity to explain why the shirt is his or her favorite and what it means to him or her.

2 Give each student a copy of the "My Favorite T-Shirt" reproducible sheet. Have the students decorate the T-shirts with drawings that include clues about who they are. They may want to include their hobbies, interests, family, or cultural heritage.

3 To display the art, hang a piece of cord or rope from one side of the room or hallway to the other side. Hang the T-shirts with clothespins for an unusual, charming display that celebrates the uniqueness of your students. After the shirts are on the line, you may want to have a contest to see how many kids can be identified from what they represented on the T-shirts. Then give each child a chance to talk about what is on his or her T-shirt.

Date Used   Notes

©TREND

My Favorite
T-Shirt

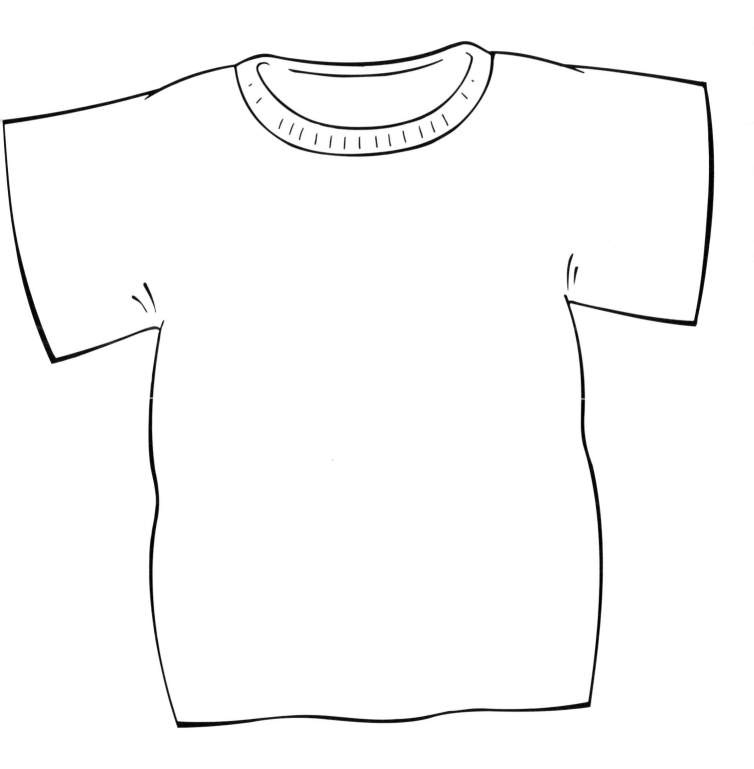

School Celebrities

Materials & Prep

- Markers
- TREND Ready Letters®

In preparation for this activity, decide on a word to use for the activity and write clues on the Ready Letters® for your students to follow. See below for more information.

Activity

This is a way to meet the important people and visit important rooms around school. Students follow clues that take them to many places around the school.

1 Decide on a word or phrase that includes one letter for each person or place you'll visit in the school. For example, if you have seven people to visit, you might choose *friends* or *welcome*.

2 Make up a clue for each person or place you want to visit. Write the clues on the back of the letters or on a separate sheet of paper. Here are some sample clues:
- This is a person that runs the school—Principal.
- This person could take my temperature or give me a bandage—Nurse.
- This person takes care of the building, so it's a safe place to learn—Custodian.
- These people make sure I have the vitamins and minerals I need to keep me healthy —Cafeteria Workers.
- This area holds the largest collection of words in the school—Media Center.
- This is a place where you hear lots of different sounds —Music Room.

3 Hide the first letter and clue in your classroom. Give the next letter, and a clue to the first person you would like to visit. Continue the process by being sure each celebrity you visit has the clue that will lead the class to the next person. By following clues to collect the letters, your students will be introduced to people and places around the building. Ask each "celebrity" to tell the class a little bit about his or her job or the particular place he or she works.

4 When the students have all the letters, they can put them together to figure out the word.

Date Used   Notes

How Do I Measure Up?

Materials & Prep

• Large roll of newsprint or butcher paper (if not in school supplies, check with your local newspaper for a free end roll of newsprint)

• Plastic links and other non-standard measuring tools

• Markers or crayons

• Rulers/measuring tapes

Activity

Students will have fun as they practice measuring skills in this artsy activity.

1 Pairs of students take turns lying down on large pieces of newsprint. Partners trace around each other, creating life-sized shapes.

2 Students then use various tools to measure the body parts—arms, feet, legs, etc.—and write the measurements on the outline. Measure with plastic links, another common math manipulative, or other non-standard units of measure.

Make this activity more challenging by including circumference measurements, such as head and waist, or by requiring students to record measurements using two different units, such as inches and centimeters.

3 Encourage the students to add fun final touches to their outlines, such as hair, clothing, and facial features.

Your students get a chance to practice both measurement and socialization skills, and the finished products look great displayed in the hallway!

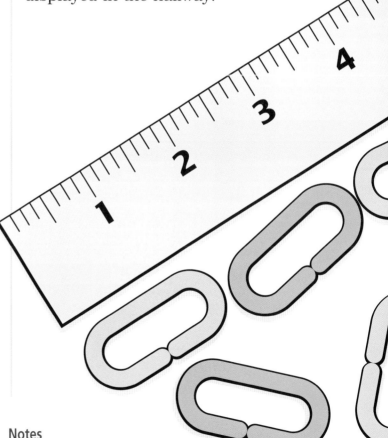

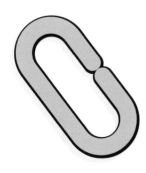

Date Used   Notes

Graduation Time Capsule

Materials & Prep

- One copy of "Time Capsule" sheet for each student
- One copy of "All About Me" sheet for each student (page 68)
- Drawing paper
- Shoe boxes
- String

Activity

This is often a favorite project with the parents. It is an excellent activity for the entire class to work on, and it will be a fun time capsule to be opened upon high school graduation.

1 At the start of the year label a shoebox for each child.

2 Send home the "Time Capsule" letter with each student. This letter will help explain the project to the parents and tell them how they can help build an exciting keepsake. Let parents know that, if they would like to add to the capsule, they are welcome to send things with their children to school or bring them in themselves.

3 What to include in the time capsule:

- Pictures of the children during the school year. Two or three pictures per student is great. Include a class picture in each capsule too.

- At least one sample of the child's art, math work, writing, and science work, as well as other academic papers.

- A copy of the "All About Me" sheet completed by the individual student.

4 At the end of the year, ask parent volunteers to wrap the boxes for safe keeping. Attach a ribbon to each with a tag that says: "To be opened on _____'s high school graduation day."

Tips:
- Many pictures will likely feature more than one student. It saves in the long run to make double prints.

- For the class photo take a roll of pictures and get double prints rather than making reprints of just one photo.

- Ask parents to donate film and help with developing costs.

By the end of the year you will have collected many different important momentos of each child's year.

Date Used   Notes

_____   _____

_____   _____

Time Capsule

___/___/___

Dear Parent or Guardian,

Your child is a part of a very special class, the graduating class of _____.

To commemorate this year and the graduation event, we are planning a special project. We are making a time capsule for each child, to be opened when he or she graduates from high school. By the end of this year, the capsule will include a picture of your child in ____ grade, writing samples, and other surprises.

To accomplish our plans, we are asking for some help from you:

1. Please send a shoe box (also known as a time capsule) to school. Label the box with your child's name.

2. Please write your child a personal letter for him or her to open at high school graduation. Date it and tell him or her anything you wish. Please seal it and put your child's name on the outside of the envelope.

3. You could also include an artifact, such as a family picture, a list of things your child has done this year, or whatever you think would be fun to have inside the time capsule.

Please have your letter and box to school by _____. Thank you for your help in making this special project possible.

Sincerely,

All About Me

All about me in the year _____

1. I like to eat _____

2. I like to play _____

3. On T.V. I watch _____

4. My favorite movie is _____

5. My best friend is _____

6. When I grow up I want to be a _____

   _____

7. On separate pieces of paper trace around your feet and your hands, one at a time.

8. Use a string to measure your height and tape it here.

Temperature Graph

Materials & Prep

- Thermometer
- Butcher paper
- Markers/crayons
- A device for finding out about the weather each day (see ideas below)

Activity

Keeping track of the temperature is a great on-going activity. It provides experience in graphing, comparing, and gathering data from many sources.

1 Before you get started determine how you will verify the temperature each day.

- Obtain a local weather phone number.
- Watch a weather channel on TV.
- Find an Internet site that gives current temperature.
- Check in a newspaper. (It will list previous day's temperatures.)
- Have a thermometer installed outside the building.

Talk to the students about weather and exchange stories about times when it was very hot or very cold. Show them a thermometer and discuss how to read it. Ask the students if they know why the weather changes like it does. (*Because of the tilt of the earth during different seasons, parts of the earth are closer to the sun than others. For example, during North America's winter it is tilted further away from the sun causing colder weather. At that same time, South America is closer to the sun and is in its warmer, summer season.*)

2 On butcher paper make a graph with every ten degrees labeled across the bottom in a different color. Label the left scale with the days of the month.

3 Pick a convenient and consistent time to check the temperature each day.

4 Color in the square on the graph above the temperature of the day.

5 Predict the color that will "win" each month. As the year goes on it's amazing to see the guesses improve.

Date Used	Notes

It's Me All Over

Materials & Prep

- Sheets of butcher paper the size of each student
- Copies of the parent letter
- Other materials as provided at students' homes

Activity

Using a full size outline of each child as a background is a fun way to collect and display information about the child.

1 Provide butcher paper the approximate size of each student. Any color or combination of colors works well.

2 Have student partners or classroom volunteers trace around each of the children as they lie on the paper.

3 Roll up and put a rubber band around each sheet for the students to take home with a letter from you. The letter may read like this:

Dear Parent or Guardian,

The children in our class have drawn body outlines of themselves. Please work with your child to decorate the outline to reflect his or her personality.

Consider using pictures from magazines, pictures your child drew, or actual photos to attach to the outline. Then have your child write a caption under each picture that explains a little bit about himself or herself.

Send the completed outline back to school by

_____.

We will take care of this project and return it to you after a few weeks, but please do not send in any pictures or photos that cannot be replaced. This is a great way for us to get to know your child. Thank you for your help.

Sincerely,

As the outlines come back, have the children explain them. Then display the outlines in your classroom or in the hallway outside the room.

Date Used   Notes

Class Phone Book

Materials & Prep

- One copy of a permission slip for each student
- Pencils
- Black felt-tip markers
- Drawing paper

Activity

This activity is a favorite every year. The students end up with their very own phone book and you have a quick assessment of their letter and number writing skills and their drawing capabilities.

1 Send home a letter asking parents for permission to publish the students' phone number in your class phone book. If there is an open house or orientation early in the year, have a permission sheet there for parents to sign.

2 When parents have given permission, have each child write his or her name and phone number near the top of a half sheet of drawing paper. If any parents have not given permission to use the phone number, the children should only write their names on the paper.

3 The space remaining on the paper is for self-portraits. Have students draw in pencil first and then trace over their portraits with a black felt-tip pen.

4 Make a cover for the phone book by having each child draw a small face to decorate the cover.

5 After the students complete their pages, arrange to have the book printed on the school's copy machine or at a local copy center. If you'd like, plan a field trip for students to watch some of the printing.

Make enough copies of the phone book for class members and extra copies to give to any new students that join your class. Now teachers, parents, and students can stay in touch with people from the class.

FACT: The first words spoken over the telephone were, "Watson, please come over here. I want you."

Date Used   Notes

Friendly Food

Materials & Prep

- Friendship bread recipe and ingredients
- Chart paper
- One quart-sized plastic bag for each student
- Markers
- Large plastic bowl
- Wooden spoon
- Fruit and store-bought desserts brought by students
- Copies of "Friendly Food" reproducible

Activity

Students cooperate to prepare a friendly, delicious lunch.

1 Start working on your friendship lunch ten days in advance by starting friendship bread. This recipe requires a starter. Ask around to see if someone has some, or order from Armchair World at (310) 477-8960. Copy the recipe on chart paper and explain the importance of following the directions carefully. If you would like, add a science experiment to this activity by letting students make two batches —one following the recipe exactly, and one altering it, such as using metal utensils. Then compare the results.

2 Send a letter home to parents explaining that your class will be enjoying a friendship lunch in ten days. While students need not bring lunch money or cold lunch that day, they do need to bring one piece of fruit and a gift-wrapped individual dessert.

3 On the designated day, bake the bread as directed and make a friendship fruit salad by preparing and combining the fruit students brought from home. During this preparation, display a piece of rotten fruit, explaining that it can ruin the whole bowl of fruit, just as one student can ruin an experience for the whole class. Have extra fruit and dessert on hand in case any students forget to bring items from home.

4 After enjoying the fruit salad and bread, kids can participate in a dessert exchange. Be sensitive to any food allergies students may have.

5 Send each student home with containers with equal amounts of friendship dough starter and copies of the bread recipe.

This delicious activity will be fondly remembered for a long time!

Date Used   Notes

Friendly Food

Amish Friendship Bread
Makes 2 loaves

Day 1: Put live starter in a bowl.

Days 2–5: Stir with a wooden spoon.

Day 6: Add one cup each of flour, sugar, and milk. Stir with a wooden spoon.

Days 7–9: Stir with a wooden spoon.

Day 10: Stir in one cup each of flour, sugar, and milk. Put one cup into each of three separate containers, such as margarine tubs or quart-sized plastic bags.* Give one cup of this batter and a copy of the recipe to each of three friends. To the balance of the batter, mix in one cup oil, three eggs, ½ cup milk, and one teaspoon vanilla.

In a separate bowl, mix one cup flour, one cup sugar, 1 ½ teaspoons baking powder, ½ teaspoon salt, ½ teaspoon baking soda, one cup chopped nuts, two teaspoons cinnamon, and one (about 5 oz.) box of instant vanilla pudding.

Add the dry ingredients to the wet ingredients and pour the mixture into two greased loaf pans. Bake at 325° F for one hour.

Do not use metal bowls or utensils. Use plastic or glazed ceramic bowls, and do not refrigerate.

*When making this recipe with your class, you may want to put a small amount of starter into containers for each student to take home along with the recipe.

The Doorbell Rang Revisited

Materials & Prep

- A copy of *The Doorbell Rang,* by Pat Hutchins
- 150 small counters (i.e. poker chips, paper clips, bottle caps, pennies)
- 4 to 6 dozen cookies
- 1 tray
- Paper plates
- Costumes (optional)

Activity

Students will use a popular picture book to practice math story problems.

1 Read the book, *The Doorbell Rang,* to the class. In this book, a child's mother makes a batch of cookies for two children to share. As the doorbell keeps ringing and more and more friends come to visit, the kids discover that they each have fewer cookies when dividing them evenly. At the end, Grandma saves the day by bringing over a fresh batch of cookies.

2 After reading the book, explain that the class will be acting out the story.

You can make this as elaborate or as simple as you choose in terms of costumes, sets, props, etc. However, in order to focus on the division skills, it is crucial to have a tray, some plates, and counters to represent the cookies. There are fourteen characters in the book, so you may need to split your class in half and perform the play with two separate casts so that everyone is involved.

3 You can be the narrator the first time while the students largely mime their parts. This way students can focus on figuring out how to divide the cookies.

4 After the first run-through, create a chart with the class to determine how many cookies Mom made, how many each character got, and how many cookies Grandma made. Add up the total number of cookies needed to accurately recreate the story.

5 The following day, bring the correct number of cookies to school. You will need four to six dozen, depending on the size of your class. You may want to ask parents to send some cookies. Let your class perform the play again, this time with real cookies.

When the play has been completed, throw a cast party, and this time eat the cookies.

Date Used   Notes

©TREND

Me Books

Materials & Prep

- White construction paper
- Pencils
- Crayons/markers/colored pencils
- One photo of each student
- Book binding materials (brads, staples, darning needles and yarn, or a book-binding machine)

Activity

In this fun writing project, students write books about a favorite subject, themselves. Then they will have the opportunity to share the books with the class.

1 Brainstorm a list of important items to know about people in order to get to know them. Include who else is in their family, interesting hobbies, what he or she looks like, etc. This will be the list of topics that your students will write about in the Me Books.

2 When you have a list, let each student pair it down to the 5-10 most important items. Then let them start writing, creating a book that is as unique as they are. Have students plan for one page for each topic. Encourage them to bring in any items that they may want to include, such as photographs, ticket stubs, programs, or other relatively flat souvenirs.

3 In addition to writing and attaching personal mementos, students can illustrate their topics with drawings, computer graphics, or photo collages. Let students create book covers using photos of themselves.

4 When the books are complete, demonstrate the bookbinding techniques that you have available. Let the students choose one method to bind their books.

5 Finally, devote some time to letting students share their books with the class. Their pride will come shining through!

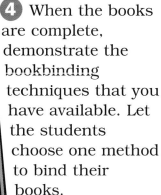

Date Used   Notes

Stump the Teacher

Materials & Prep

- Index cards
- Pens/pencils
- Stopwatch
- Pretend money
- Four of five sets of textbooks and/or workbooks from your students' previous grade level

Activity

You won't believe how students enjoy reviewing the previous year's curriculum in this activity!

1 Obtain four or five copies of the curricular materials that the students used the previous school year, such as textbooks and workbooks.

2 Divide your students into the same number of small groups as the number of subject areas you wish to review. For instance, if you want to work on spelling, math, social studies, and science, you would split your class into four groups. Give each group five index cards.

3 Tell your students that they are to review the curricular materials and write five questions, one per index card, in an effort to stump the teacher. They will be eager to review materials in order to accomplish this task!

4 Ask teams to rank their questions in order of difficulty and to write $100.00 on the back of the easiest one, up to $500.00 on the most difficult question. When all teams are done, arrange cards in a column from easiest to hardest.

Math	Language	Spelling	Social Studies	Science
$100	$100	$100	$100	$100
$200	$200	$200	$200	$200
$300	$300	$300	$300	$300
$400	$400	$400	$400	$400
$500	$500	$500	$500	$500

5 Choose a student to be the host and another to be the banker, and let the games begin! As you answer questions, require the team that wrote the question to find the correct answer in the materials to check your answer. When you get an answer right, you receive the amount of money written on the back of the card. If you get an answer wrong, you must pay the amount written on the back of the card.

6 Students can add up your winnings at the end of the game.

Later in the year, create a similar game for your students to play. Challenge them to earn more than you did!

Date Used   Notes

3-D Map

Materials & Prep

- A large piece of white newsprint (approximately 5' x 5')
- Rulers
- Construction paper
- Tempera paint
- Paint brushes
- Markers/crayons/colored pencils
- Scissors
- Small, clean milk cartons

Activity

Students will get valuable mapping experience while they learn about their community. Explain to the class that they will be making a map of the neighborhood.

1 Place the newsprint on the floor or on a table. Have everyone gather around the paper. Start with the school in the center of the paper. Discuss the shape of the building. Have one or more students draw it, or find a box to represent the school. Let students take turns decorating and labeling the school.

2 Draw the streets surrounding the school. You may choose to precede this part of the activity with a short walking tour of the neighborhood. Label the streets appropriately.

3 Students can use individual milk cartons to represent the other buildings located around the school. Encourage students to paint and label cartons so that these buildings look like those they might see in the area. With your help, they can place these in the appropriate spots on the map.

4 Finally, the class can add parks, bodies of water, railroad tracks, and greenery.

Display this 3-D map on a table for a few weeks so students can have a chance to examine their work.

Date Used   Notes

Cookie Count

Materials & Prep

- Chocolate chip cookies
- Your favorite chocolate chip cookie recipe and ingredients
- 2 large mixing bowls
- Measuring cups
- Measuring spoons
- 2 wooden spoons
- Oven

Activity

Use this delicious activity to practice estimation, measuring, division, and averaging skills.

1 Hold up a chocolate chip cookie for the class to see. Ask students to estimate how many chocolate chips are in that cookie and record each student's estimate on the board.

2 Give each student a chocolate chip cookie to look at closely. Allow students to revise the estimate made before, now that they have had a closer look at a similar cookie.

3 Tell the students to eat the cookies carefully, trying to count the number of chocolate chips as they go. Then let them make more revisions of the estimates. Compare the estimates at the three stages.

4 Make a batch of chocolate chip cookies with the class. Allow students to take turns doing the measuring.

5 When it's time to add the package of chocolate chips, ask the students for ways to determine how many chips are in the bag. Record the estimated number of chips in the bag, and proceed with baking the cookies.

6 When the cookies are baked, count how many cookies there are and record that number. See if your students can figure out how many chips are in each cookie. How does this number compare to the previous estimates? The next step is for students to eat one more cookie, again counting the number of chips as they eat.

7 Show students how they can average all of the estimates they came up with to arrive at a "best guess." To find this average, add all estimates and divide by the number of estimates made. This average number of chips in a chocolate chip cookie is a "best guess."

This activity, which includes the popular activities of cooking and eating, provides excellent concrete experiences with estimation.

Date Used   Notes

Go Me! Pennants

Materials & Prep

- Paper, fabric, or cardboard pennants (see illustrations)
- Markers, paints, colored pencils, and/or crayons
- Scissors
- Glue/paste
- Fabric markers or paints
- Glitter
- Fabric scraps
- Old magazines to cut apart
- Other types of media (optional)

Activity

Creating "Go Me! Pennants" is a fun way for students to introduce themselves to their new classmates, teacher, and the school. This activity will invite each student to create a pennant that will show everyone who they are and what makes them special.

1 Tell students that they will be creating a pennant that will tell people about themselves. Pose some questions that they might want to "answer" on their pennant. What is your favorite food? What sports do you play? What do you look like? What is your best subject? Who are the people in your family?

2 Lay out the paper, cardboard, or fabric pennants. Allow students to choose the materials they will use to make their pennants.

3 When students have completed this project, there are several ways to share their masterpieces.

- Give students the option to talk about their pennants in front of the class.

- Hold one pennant up at a time and have students guess the significance of items pictured.

- Hang the pennants in the room or hall for everyone to see.

As proud fans might display the pennants of teams they follow or root for, you too can display the pennants of your students who will make you proud this year.

Date Used   Notes

Index